Healing
Your Heart

A PROMPTED JOURNAL FOR PREGNANCY LOSS

KAYLIN R. STATEN

HOURGLASS
MEDIA

Huntington, WV

HOURGLASS
MEDIA

Hourglass Media
Huntington, WV

First Hourglass Media hardback and eBook edition 2021.

Print ISBN 978-0-9968233-6-4
eBook ISBN 978-0-9968233-5-7

Library of Congress Control Number PENDING

Manufactured in the United States of America

www.hourglassmedia.company
www.kaylinstaten.com

Other Works By Kaylin R. Staten:

From Granny's Kitchen
A Broken Bottle of Lovely Longings
Plastic Cupcakes

About the Author:

Kaylin R. Staten, APR, is an award-winning, accredited public relations practitioner and writer based in Huntington, WV, with 18 years of professional communications experience. As CEO and founder of Hourglass Media, she uses her compassionate spirit and expertise to delve into the heart of clients' stories. She is a recovering perfectionist, mental health advocate, wife, boy + cat mom, and Leia Organa aficionado. After having two miscarriages, she aims to help other parents who have struggled with similar losses through storytelling and authentic narratives.

✦ DEDICATION ✦

"Somewhere over the rainbow, way up high.
There's a land that I heard of once in a lullaby."
From "The Wizard of Oz."

This journal and all subsequent narratives in this book are
dedicated to the two little lives we lost.
I can't wait to hold you both in my arms someday.

June 4, 2019
April 20, 2021

This journal is also dedicated to my rainbow baby, Luke.
You have and always will be the rainbow between two storms.
My love for you knows no bounds.

I love you all,
Mom

CONTENTS

PROLOGUE:
INTRODUCTION & MY STORY
Page 1

CHAPTER I:
YOUR PREGNANCY
Page 9

CHAPTER II:
THE MISCARRIAGE PROCESS
Page 19

CHAPTER III:
YOUR CHILD'S MEMORY
Page 35

CHAPTER IV:
THE FIRST 12 WEEKS
Page 45

CHAPTER V:
MONTHLY LETTERS TO YOUR CHILD
Page 109

EPILOGUE:
OTHER NOTES & RESOURCES
Page 128

✦ INTRODUCTION ✦

If you picked up this journal, you are grieving.

One in four pregnancies will end in a loss. Although this isn't how I would want to meet you, I am glad you're here. I know you are hurting, and I know you have an innate desire to keep your child's legacy alive. It's hard to make sense of how you are feeling and how this experience will shape your entire life from this moment forward.

My hope is that this journal, when complemented with other healing practices, can help you feel like you can survive this darkest hour. I know you don't feel that way now, and you will begin to heal at your own pace. Each section will allow you to fill in the details of your own experience, from how you felt when you discovered you were pregnant to when your miscarriage process ended to the present day. If you're actively miscarrying right now or a certain amount of time has passed, this journal will allow you to share your memories of your child, chronicle your weekly feelings, and get all of your thoughts on paper (or screen).

Grief is complicated, and many times, we want to push away how we feel. We compartmentalize our grief into silos to deal with on a "better" day, when we have "more time" or "feel like it." I urge you to consider not waiting to get to the heart of this story. It's important, and it belongs to you and your child. You deserve for it to see the light of day.

I'm not a medical or mental health professional. While I am not an expert on the clinical side, I've been where you are. I am still on my own miscarriage journey, and I aim to help others by sharing their own child loss stories. What I can do is support you through my own personal narrative, resources, and these journal prompts.

-

**Sending you love, light, and healing,
Kaylin**

MY STORY

The First Miscarriage
First Published in Harness Magazine on September 6, 2019

I know grief. I've lost people close to me, and I thought I knew grief like the back of my hand. Now, however, grief has a name, and it was revealed to me recently as I felt like my heart was crushing inside my chest.

Grief, to me, was exacerbated by the loss of my child on June 4, 2019.

I have gone back and forth as to if I should reveal something so private to the world. In this case, my advocacy and desire to help others outweigh all the cons. So, here is my story about my miscarriage. This is the heaviest my heart has ever felt in my 30 years on this earth. So many Band-Aids cover my heart, from childhood sadnesses to present-day heartaches; however, nothing compared to this.

On Monday, June 3, 2019, I just felt different. Sure, it was the typical symptoms, from a sore lower back to odd and frequent mood swings. I just felt pregnant. I had an allergist appointment an hour away, so I had a lot of time to think on the road–and a lot of time to plot if and when I was going to purchase a pregnancy test.

I stopped at a Dollar General on the way home to buy a First Response pregnancy test. The nervousness I felt came from an aura of excitable hope. I stood in line and thought, "I remember when a positive pregnancy test would have sent me into panic." Instead, I felt calm and collected. I handed the male cashier the pregnancy test card, and he handed me an actual box from behind the counter. Ten years ago, I would have been mortified, but I felt empowered because I just knew I was going to be a mom.

I drove home and immediately took the test. When a faint positive line stood proud and true beside the right line, elation filled my lungs and every part of my being. I had never seen a second line on any previous test, so I knew this meant something. I waited until my husband came home from work to tell him, but the wait nearly exhausted me. So, I wrote. I wrote about the excitement and fear I felt about being a mom.

"I'm about to vomit just talking about it here because Jared doesn't know yet. No one knows but me, God, my cats, and my journal. I'm still skeptical, but I have a feeling. My intuition tells me I'm pregnant. If I end up having a period (albeit late), I'll still think I was pregnant. I don't want to talk about a miscarriage, but I have to be realistic. ... I don't want to jinx myself. I have just dreamed of having a [girl name] or [boy name] forever."

MY STORY

My husband Jared and I talked about it that evening in a happy haze, and we started to mentally prepare for the changes that would ensue in our lives, from random pregnancy craving errand runs to preparing a nursery (leaving him without his own space for the time being). I started reading What To Expect When You're Expecting, and I fell asleep protectively holding my belly. I even started talking to my stomach the first day. My child was the size of a poppy seed, yet I knew I would do anything for that growing life inside my belly.

The next day, I woke up and took a pregnancy test again, my fifth or so one since the day before. (I am obsessive-compulsive, after all.) Jared left for work, and I even looked at him differently as the father of my child. My heart swooned, and I knew my child had the best dad in the universe. I had made a doctor's appointment the day before, so I tried to work until my afternoon appointment. No such luck because I was anxious and exhausted. I decided to go back to sleep until I had to get ready for my appointment. I woke up, went to the bathroom, and saw blood. I won't get into any details, but I will say this: It was not normal.

I called to cancel my appointment, and the tears began to flow as soon as I ended the call. I paced back and forth. I prayed to God. I sat by the toilet and wept for my lost child. I had to say something, so I said a eulogy on the tile floor, surrounded by two supportive cats. To this day, I cannot describe the devastation I felt then and still feel.

"How quickly things can change in 24 hours. I was elated at this point yesterday, and now, depression has taken its familiar throne. I do not feel like writing. I would rather be under the covers in Jared's old fraternity T-shirt with the ceiling fan on high and watching something mindless. But, that won't do anything but feed the depression, anxiety, and fear. And it will do my child a disservice. Because, yes, I lost my child today."

That was our child. I have always wanted to be a mom, and when I met my husband, I knew he was the one I would share that dream with. All of that hope was gone as swiftly as it arrived, replaced by the aching and burning of a broken heart and emptiness in the pit of my stomach. I felt like something was already missing inside me.

But, the love is still there and will always remain in my heart.

After several trips to the doctor, and being poked and prodded beyond belief, what I knew deep in my bones to be the truth was confirmed: I had a very early miscarriage. The sensitivity of today's pregnancy tests detects the hCG hormone much earlier than in previous years. If I hadn't felt the changes to my body, missed my period, and taken a test, I would have never known and thought it was business as usual.

MY STORY

For some reason, I was meant to know. I'm still searching for that reason, but I have faith that I will know God's plan eventually. I have to have faith, because without it, I would be an empty shell.

When my child's due date (2/10/20) arrives, I cannot predict how I will feel. Multiple emotions, I'm sure. What I do know is this: In my heart, my baby and I will be together forever.

If you have a first-trimester miscarriage, especially a chemical pregnancy, you may feel like it doesn't compare to other people's pregnancy or stillborn-birth losses. I believe that once the point of conception occurs, the life forming inside a woman is indeed a baby. I know other people disagree, and if so, this blog post isn't for you anyway. So, it doesn't matter if you lost your baby at 5 weeks or 5 months. It was your child. The only difference is the time you were able to spend with your growing child.

The could-have-beens gut punch me when I think about them. Was my child a boy or girl? What would he/she have been like? How would I have felt when I heard the first heartbeat, saw the first image, looked at his/her face for the first time after giving birth?

It is essential to allow yourself to grieve, no matter the term of your pregnancy. I was a mother, even for a short time. I knew what it felt like to be pregnant for 24 hours, and it was a different, surreal happiness. I felt surreal happiness when I met my husband and throughout the tenure of our relationship and marriage, but this—this was something entirely exclusive to parenthood.

And it's something I will hold on to forever.

The Second Miscarriage
First Published in Harness Magazine on June 1, 2021

"This can't be happening. Not again."

Disbelief clouds my morning, introducing the old adversary of unspeakable grief. I wipe tears from my tired eyes as I attempt to make a fraction of sense as my world spirals out of control. Again. This time, I'm in a different bathroom, but the confusion and pain still reverberate all around me.

Twenty-four hours earlier, I sat in this same spot in the master bathroom, a carbon copy of minutes I had already lived. That same brand of disbelief made itself right at home in my mind then, too, but this greeted me in a different way—two blue lines formed within a three-minute span. Sobbing, my brain commenced with its all-too-familiar what-if scenarios.

MY STORY

I couldn't believe I was pregnant. In my journal entry highlighting this recent life development, I wrote, *"I was just pregnant eight months ago!!"*

I didn't expect to see a positive pregnancy test, although I knew deep in my heart that I was having early pregnancy symptoms. After having a child, you begin to notice even the most minute nuances when your body is off-kilter. This pregnancy was a result of a birth control failure, which made it all the more perplexing and shocking.

Ultimately, and in a short amount of time, I began coming to terms with this unplanned pregnancy. I started to brainstorm about how we could convert my office to the second baby's nursery. I thought about all of our son's clothes we could save, all of the boy items, and then the gender-neutral things if the baby happened to be a girl. I began to envision the first time I would lay eyes on our second child: the overwhelming feelings of eternal, unconditional love as I held him/her in my arms for the first time. Seeing my son hold his little sibling. Witnessing both of them grow up into who they were meant to be. Being a proud mother as I detailed their lives, feeling blessed to know them — let alone be their mother. This baby would have been born in December, a surprise Christmas gift we never knew would happen but loved all the same.

Those daydreams ended, and now, we will never know.

I began bleeding the evening of April 19 and lost the baby at 7:30 a.m. on April 20. I woke up to intense contraction-like cramping and bleeding, and as I tossed and turned in bed, I felt the inevitable weight of what was happening. My journal entry, raw and authentic, illustrates the emotions: "The love I will always feel circumvents any fears that I felt about having another baby. I wanted this baby. There's no doubt in my mind, despite the initial shock of an unplanned pregnancy. ... I walked into the living room and told Jared [about the bleeding]. He immediately embraced me, and having him here this time helped. I have experienced this before, and the PTSD flooded back into my consciousness. This heartache is bad enough to go through once. But twice? It's unfathomable. Deep inside my heart and gut, I knew what happened. The baby was gone."

Instead of welcoming another baby into the world, ultrasound paperwork explicitly states "infant demise." My body went through all of the motions of a miscarriage, an unfortunately familiar road I went down less than two years ago. I had to tell my husband that we lost another child as grief washed over the both of us. I forced myself to smile during virtual meetings "that I couldn't get out of" so I could maintain a sense of normalcy, carrying on when I wanted to let myself fall apart. I kept hugging my son, and he was confused when I bawled my eyes out. I floated through the days like a ghost of my former self. Exhaustion plagued me.

MY STORY

The only visual proof I have of this pregnancy is the relentless needle marks from constant bloodwork, and the pregnancy tests tucked into a box. I also have the video I made of our son as I talked to him about how he was going to be a big brother, as well as the words I wrote in my journal and iPhone chronicling my experiences throughout the process.

Coupled with such a devastating loss was the prospect of an ectopic pregnancy. Due to not being able to see anything on the ultrasound and the slow and unpredictable fluctuation of the hCG hormone in my body, my doctor couldn't definitively tell me which type of miscarriage I was experiencing. Ectopic or tubal pregnancies can have dire consequences, from the loss of a Fallopian tube to internal bleeding that leads to death. Not only was I going through the grief of losing another child to a miscarriage, but I worried for my life. I have anxious tendencies, but the fears and threats were incredibly real and increasingly valid. I didn't know if I would have to have surgery. I didn't know if I just wouldn't wake up one day because of complications. I lived in a world of unknowns for two weeks.

Now that I am out of the woods and my body is naturally handling the miscarriage, high levels of introspection hijack my mind throughout the day. I experienced my first miscarriage on June 4, 2019, and it happened to be my first-ever pregnancy. It nearly destroyed me and broke my entire heart. I worked myself to the bone and sat on the couch playing "The Elder Scrolls V: Skyrim," barely moving from either perch until I absolutely had to. My husband and I leaned on each other for support, and we wanted a child so badly. I thought it was my fault, and I wrestled with the feeling that I did something to cause the miscarriage. Perhaps I drank an ounce more coffee than I should have, or stress caused a genetic malfunction. It took me months upon months of therapy to get through this period of my life.

In early January 2020, I discovered I was pregnant again, and we didn't tell anyone until after the 12th week. We wanted to ensure that we heard his heartbeat and that he was OK. Our son was born in the midst of the pandemic in August 2020, a rainbow in the darkness.

An estimated one in four pregnancies end in miscarriage, and most miscarriages occur in the first trimester (12 weeks) of pregnancy. If a woman has a live birth, the miscarriage risk is typically lower, approximately one in 25 pregnancies. I am part of that statistic. Even if you haven't personally experienced a miscarriage, you will likely know a woman — or several — who have suffered this type of loss.

While this miscarriage broke a new piece of my heart, I am beyond blessed to have my son. I cherish the recordings of his heartbeat in utero, the ultrasound pictures, and the journey that allowed him to be here with us. So many people don't have that blessing in their fertility struggles, and I hold

MY STORY

closer to me than ever before. He is and will forever be my miracle rainbow baby. My heart aches for each person who wants a child so much but is struggling or has the hard line in the sand telling them they can't have a child. So many people experience pregnancy loss (or can't get pregnant at all), and I was meant to shed light on these struggles. This is a real issue, so many women and their partners go through, and we don't have to suffer in silence. If you have had a miscarriage or multiple losses, I am here for you. I see and hear you. And I feel your everlasting love for your babies. You aren't alone, and you don't have to struggle with this loss alone.

So many others are sharing their miscarriages, from Meghan, Duchess of Sussex, singer Christina Perri, Beyoncé, and countless others in the public eye. I want to add to the fabric of stories that change our lives. Just like with my first miscarriage, I aim to keep my children's legacies alive by telling their stories and destigmatizing miscarriage. This purpose was further intensified by a second miscarriage, the loss of another child. My life has forever been altered by these experiences, and I cannot go back to the person I used to be. Miscarriages change you.

Despite my grief, I know my two angel babies saved my life. I have never spoken about this publicly and even privately, and I won't detail every moment here. In time, this story will fill the pages of personal and professional tomes. However, now is not that time, but I do want to provide some insight into how these babies saved me. In 2013, I was at the lowest point in my life. I felt trapped by an abusive relationship, isolated from my loved ones, and felt disparagingly alone every single day. My life slowly etched itself into a fleeting shadow of what I wanted it to be. I looked in the mirror and couldn't recognize myself anymore, a gargoyle in a room of beautiful colored glass. Depressed and in great need of mental health support, I began spiraling out of control. Suddenly, I heard the voices of two children, a boy, and a girl, call me Mommy. They told me life would get better, that I would get what I deserved. I would find my soulmate and be a mother.

I get chills when I remember this moment.

I know without a shadow of a doubt that God and these two babies were with me. I hadn't met my husband yet or even fathomed becoming a mother, but this glimpse into my future allowed me to snap out of my darkest hour. This gives me solace and promise. I am a mother of three, one on Earth and two in heaven. One summer child and two winter children. I find comfort in knowing that I will hold these children someday. I am thankful for the blessing of knowing them before they grew inside me and before I carried their legacies with me every minute of every day.

Miscarriages never get easier. Losing a child, let alone two or more, is

MY STORY

something I will never get over. I won't snap out of grief. I won't forget them. I will love my children until my dying breath and then throughout eternity.

After my C-section with my son, I remember looking at the sterile white walls and ceiling tiles of the operating room and thinking, "My life is complete." My family was meant to be a family of three with two in heaven.

My musings have ultimately led me to this realization: it's OK to not have the nuclear family everyone else expects. Many of you reading this will already know this and wholeheartedly agree with the sentiment. I had to experience all of it for myself, on my own yellow brick road journey. I don't care about others' judgments or declarations of, "But, Luke will be an only child" and "I wish you would have more children." Ultimately, we learn the most profound lessons and have the most groundbreaking experiences when we figure things out on our own during periods of loss and pain.

Since I was a little girl, "Over the Rainbow" from "The Wizard of Oz" has been an illustrious piece of music that shaped my entire life. The lyrics have so many meanings for me, but now, I know my two babies are waiting for me in the "land that I heard of once in a lullaby." I have my rainbow (Luke), and my angel children are my "dreams that [I] dare to dream."

I have walked through the fires of grief and have made it on the other side before. I know I will do it all over again. I didn't expect to even be pregnant or have to grieve over the loss of another child, but my resilience and faith will pull me through oblivion. And when I make it to the other side, I will continue to treasure all three of my children.

Now, it's your turn to tell your and your baby's stories.

This journal is in honor of:

Your baby's due date:

This journal belongs to:

"I carried you for every second of your life, and I will love you for every second of mine."

AUTHOR UNKNOWN

✦ YOUR PREGNANCY ✦

These pages are undated. Fill them in as you feel up to it. You can always date them in the margins, too!

Were you trying for a baby or was this pregnancy a surprise?

Did you have any issues conceiving?

Do you have any other children? What were those pregnancies like?

What were your initial reactions when you found out you were pregnant?

What five words described how you felt in that moment?

Did you feel positive or negative emotions? Describe those here.

Did this experience match what you anticipated?

Where were you when you found out you were pregnant?
Describe the setting and any sensory details.

How many pregnancy tests did you take?

Did you tell anyone, and who did you tell and when? How did they react?

Did you have your initial doctor's appointment?

Did you have an ultrasound, hear the heartbeat, and experience other pregnancy processes?

Which pregnancy symptoms did you have?

Did you start to prepare for life with this baby? How so?

What else do you want to remember about your pregnancy journey?

More Thoughts:

✦ ANGELIC LEGACY ✦

I wish I knew you
Kissed your rosy swollen cheeks
Held you to my heart after birth
But you weren't meant for this earth.

I couldn't save you then
Or forget you to save you even now
As your sibling grows inside me
I'll never forget your angelic legacy.

-

Kaylin R. Staten
February 7, 2020

THE MISCARRIAGE PROCESS

"Write hard
and clear
about what hurts."

ERNEST HEMINGWAY

THE MISCARRIAGE PROCESS

These pages are undated. Fill them in as you feel up to it. You can always date them in the margins, too!

How did you know your were miscarrying? What day was it?

How far along were you?

Where were you when you began to miscarry?

Talk about your miscarriage process.

Which miscarriage indicators made you begin to worry?

_____

_____

_____

_____

_____

_____

_____

_____

_____

_____

_____

_____

_____

_____

_____

Did you experience any physical pain, and if so, how did you combat it?

_____

_____

_____

_____

_____

_____

_____

How did you feel, emotionally?

How did you partner react, or if you don't have a partner, how did someone close to you react?

Did you feel supported by your partner, loved ones, medical professionals during this process? Why or why not?

Which types of support worked best for you during this time?

Did your doctor explain your options to you?

Did your doctor and the medical staff show you empathy?

When you found out you were miscarrying, how did the next 24 hours go?
Did you stay home, talk with a loved one, proceed as "normal," etc.?

Did you take any time off work? Why or why not?

Was this your first miscarriage?

How did your partner (or someone close to you) handle the loss?

How do you handle grief? How are you handling grief with regards to this loss?

Do you blame yourself?

Has anyone close to you ever had a miscarriage?

Did you have any indication of what the miscarriage experience would be like?

What types of medical procedures did you have to have during your miscarriage process? Did you experience your miscarriage naturally or have a procedure like a D&C?

Did anyone reach out to you to offer help during this time (a meal, invitations to talk if needed/wanted, etc.)?

Have you had to deal with anything you considered unhelpful at this time?
What is triggering you?

When did you know the miscarriage process was over?

How did you feel about the finality of that moment?

What else do you want to say about your miscarriage process?

More Thoughts:

More Thoughts:

PORCELAIN EULOGY

A melancholy sun illuminates my world
As storm clouds discourage my soul
Tears ravage like thunder
Despair rippling into each crevice
Goodbyes breaking into crystal heartbeats
that never were.

I gave you my whole heart for 24 hours
My little miracle in a faint line
A five-week-old poppy seed mapped out in a
lifetime of stars
Until the blood moon eclipsed all hope
And all I had left was a five-minute porcelain
eulogy.

-

Kaylin R. Staten
June 4, 2019

✦ YOUR CHILD'S MEMORY ✦

"Take your
broken heart
and turn it
into art."

CARRIE FISHER

YOUR CHILD'S MEMORY

These pages are undated. Fill them in as you feel up to it. You can always date them in the margins, too!

Did you always imagine you would be a mom? Why did you want to be a mom?

In your eyes, what are five qualities of a good mom?

How did you want to exhibit those qualities with this child?

What did you envision for your child?

How do you imagine your child when you think of him or her? Did you know the sex of the baby, and did he/she have a name?

If the baby doesn't have a name, do you want to name him/her? Why or why not?

Which personality traits do you think your baby would have had?

What do you think your child would have looked like?

How did you imagine your child interacting with other loved ones?

If you were far enough along, did you feel the baby move? How did that make you feel?

Did you have a funeral or some type of remembrance ceremony for your child?

When you think of your child, what do you want to remember?

What do you find comfort in knowing?

What are some of your regrets?

What makes you the saddest about not having your child here with you?

Write a eulogy for your child here.

More Thoughts:

More Thoughts:

10 THINGS THAT ✦ CAN HELP DURING ✦ A MISCARRIAGE

1. Allow yourself to feel how you feel in the moment. Let the tears flow, stay in bed if you want, talk about the miscarriage and your baby.
2. Find an outlet that works for you. Write, talk with your partner, go to therapy, find a support group, or do whatever works for you.
3. Practice self-care and self-love. That could look like a good skincare routine or playing video games in your spare time for a straight week.
4. Write letters to your child to help you work through your grief and keep your child's legacy alive.
5. If someone isn't being supportive, it's OK to temporarily (or permanently, depending on the situation) distance yourself from negativity.
6. It's also OK to realize that you have triggers and to not put yourself in those situations. There's a time to face triggers and a time to take a break from being strong.
7. Take as much time as you need. Take some bereavement time off work, don't attend a major event if you're not up to it, get food delivered instead of cooking.
8. Use your grief for good. When and if you are comfortable, help others going through the same type of loss. Your empathy and active listening can mean the world to someone else.
9. Realize that your pregnancy loss is not your fault.
10. Know that you are a mother. ❤

✦ **THE FIRST 12 WEEKS** ✦

"A mother is never defined by the number of children you can see, but by the love that she holds in her heart."

FRANCHESHA COX

FIVE STAGES OF GRIEF

Denial: This initial stage is when you feel shocked -- or maybe you feel nothing at all. You seem to float through each moment and could experience an out-of-body sensation. You don't believe what your senses are relaying to you and you are in full fight-or-flight survival mode. You don't delve into your feelings and push them to the side.

Anger: Once you begin to process your emotions, anger is usually one of the first emotions that pop into your head and daily life. You could be angry that this happened to you or that you had to experience the loss of a child, while others have healthy, happy children. You're mad that you can't have that, too, and you often lash out at triggers at this stage.

Bargaining: This could present itself in various ways, but bargaining often takes the form of promising to not do something negative in order to achieve a positive outcome. You manifest your own world of what-ifs and if-onlys. You focus on what could have been done differently to achieve a different outcome. As a mother, you likely would do anything for your child and wish you could in this situation, too.

Depression: The fourth stage brings intense periods of sadness, regret, and longing for the child you lost. You may find it hard to sleep, eat, get out of bed in the morning, go the sleep at night, take care of basic needs, associate with the outside world, get through the workday, and more. This is a normal response once you realize that your child is gone. This can happen at any point during the miscarriage or loss process.

Acceptance: This is where you realize that your child is gone, and although you will never be OK with that, you are able to move forward in your grief journey. You continue to evolve, although it looks a little different now. You may want to help others who have gone through something similar as you are learning to live without your child here on earth with you. You start to adjust to your new "normal," which looks different to everyone.

Learn more about each stage here: www.grief.com/the-five-stages-of-grief.

EXAMPLES OF GRIEF

During my first miscarriage, I went to the grief stages this way:

- **Denial:** "Maybe my body is wrong. If I go to the doctor and take tests, maybe it will show that I am still pregnant." I went to the grocery store two hours later like everything was "normal." But, who wears sunglasses inside to cover up tear-swollen eyes? This girl.
- **Anger:** "Why did this happen to me, when other women can get pregnant so easily? I tried to do everything right, and this still happened."
- **Bargaining:** "Maybe if I wouldn't have had that extra cup of coffee, I wouldn't have lost the baby."
- **Depression:** "I will never get over this. I won't be the same person, and I don't want to be anyway." These actions ensued: sleeping way more than usual, sitting on the couch for hours physically feeling glued to the couch, no interest in anything, crying, anxiety/panic attacks, feelings of hopelessness, having to force myself to eat.
- **Acceptance/Meaning:** I still think about this baby every day. While I miss him/her, I know nothing was my fault. Sometimes, it just happens this way."

The second time, I handled grief in this way:

- **Denial:** "I know what happened the first time, but there is no way this is happening again. When I go to the doctor, I will see the baby on the ultrasound, and things will be fine." *ignores contraction-like cramping, bleeding, and fatigue to the best of my ability.
- **Anger:** "Why did I even have to go through this again? I wasn't even trying to get pregnant, and this happened."
- **Bargaining:** "If I wouldn't have taken ibuprofen before I knew I was pregnant, I may still be pregnant."
- **Depression:** "My body is broken. I have had two miscarriages and a high-risk pregnancy. My body just doesn't like to be pregnant, so I give up." All I wanted to do was revert to my first-miscarriage comfort zone: play "Skyrim" all day, eat comfort foods, and shut out the world. I did have my son to take care of, though, so that helped me through.
- **Acceptance/Meaning:** I haven't reached this fully yet, but I aim to help others who have gone through any type of miscarriage or child loss. I know this child is gone, but I am still struggling."

THE FIRST 12 WEEKS: WEEK ONE

DATE:

How do you feel this week? Circle one (or several).

Write about how you feel.

Have your basic needs been met this week?

How are you handling depression or any other chronic or situational
health-related issues?

Did you have any triggers this week? What are you doing to cope?

What word describes you this week?

Which stage of grief are you in? Describe the stage.

What has been a challenge for you this week?

Where do you find solace?

What are some of your healthy coping strategies? How are you healing?

What are some of your unhealthy coping strategies? How would you like to change those, if you have the desire to change them?

Are you taking some time for self-care? If so, what are you doing? If not, what has prevented you from taking care of yourself?

What are five things you're thankful for this week?

Do you feel like yourself this week?

What would you like to tell your baby this week?

Other Thoughts:

THE FIRST 12 WEEKS: WEEK TWO

DATE:

How do you feel this week? Circle one (or several).

Write about how you feel.

Have your basic needs been met this week?

*How are you handling depression or any other chronic or situational
health-related issues?*

Did you have any triggers this week? What are you doing to cope?

What word describes you this week?

Which stage of grief are you in? Describe the stage.

What has been a challenge for you this week?

Where do you find solace?

What are some of your healthy coping strategies? How are you healing?

What are some of your unhealthy coping strategies? How would you like to change those, if you have the desire to change them?

Are you taking some time for self-care? If so, what are you doing? If not, what has prevented you from taking care of yourself?

What are five things you're thankful for this week?

Do you feel like yourself this week?

What would you like to tell your baby this week?

Other Thoughts:

THE FIRST 12 WEEKS: WEEK THREE

DATE:

How do you feel this week? Circle one (or several).

😊 😌 😐 😒 😭 😶

Write about how you feel.

Have your basic needs been met this week?

*How are you handling depression or any other chronic or situational
health-related issues?*

Did you have any triggers this week? What are you doing to cope?

What word describes you this week?

Which stage of grief are you in? Describe the stage.

What has been a challenge for you this week?

Where do you find solace?

What are some of your healthy coping strategies? How are you healing?

What are some of your unhealthy coping strategies? How would you like to change those, if you have the desire to change them?

Are you taking some time for self-care? If so, what are you doing? If not, what has prevented you from taking care of yourself?

What are five things you're thankful for this week?

Do you feel like yourself this week?

What would you like to tell your baby this week?

Other Thoughts:

THE FIRST 12 WEEKS: WEEK FOUR

DATE:

How do you feel this week? Circle one (or several).

😊 😌 😐 😒 😭 😳

Write about how you feel.

Have your basic needs been met this week?

*How are you handling depression or any other chronic or situational
health-related issues?*

Did you have any triggers this week? What are you doing to cope?

What word describes you this week?

Which stage of grief are you in? Describe the stage.

What has been a challenge for you this week?

Where do you find solace?

What are some of your healthy coping strategies? How are you healing?

What are some of your unhealthy coping strategies? How would you like to change those, if you have the desire to change them?

Are you taking some time for self-care? If so, what are you doing? If not, what has prevented you from taking care of yourself?

What are five things you're thankful for this week?

Do you feel like yourself this week?

What would you like to tell your baby this week?

Other Thoughts:

THE FIRST 12 WEEKS: WEEK FIVE

DATE:

How do you feel this week? Circle one (or several).

Write about how you feel.

Have your basic needs been met this week?

How are you handling depression or any other chronic or situational health-related issues?

Did you have any triggers this week? What are you doing to cope?

What word describes you this week?

Which stage of grief are you in? Describe the stage.

What has been a challenge for you this week?

Where do you find solace?

What are some of your healthy coping strategies? How are you healing?

What are some of your unhealthy coping strategies? How would you like to change those, if you have the desire to change them?

Are you taking some time for self-care? If so, what are you doing? If not, what has prevented you from taking care of yourself?

What are five things you're thankful for this week?

Do you feel like yourself this week?

What would you like to tell your baby this week?

Other Thoughts:

THE FIRST 12 WEEKS: WEEK SIX

DATE:

How do you feel this week? Circle one (or several).

Write about how you feel.

Have your basic needs been met this week?

How are you handling depression or any other chronic or situational health-related issues?

Did you have any triggers this week? What are you doing to cope?

What word describes you this week?

Which stage of grief are you in? Describe the stage.

What has been a challenge for you this week?

Where do you find solace?

What are some of your healthy coping strategies? How are you healing?

What are some of your unhealthy coping strategies? How would you like to change those, if you have the desire to change them?

Are you taking some time for self-care? If so, what are you doing? If not, what has prevented you from taking care of yourself?

What are five things you're thankful for this week?

Do you feel like yourself this week?

What would you like to tell your baby this week?

Other Thoughts:

THE FIRST 12 WEEKS: WEEK SEVEN

DATE:

How do you feel this week? Circle one (or several).

😊 😌 😐 😒 😭 😶

Write about how you feel.

Have your basic needs been met this week?

How are you handling depression or any other chronic or situational health-related issues?

Did you have any triggers this week? What are you doing to cope?

What word describes you this week?

Which stage of grief are you in? Describe the stage.

What has been a challenge for you this week?

Where do you find solace?

What are some of your healthy coping strategies? How are you healing?

What are some of your unhealthy coping strategies? How would you like to change those, if you have the desire to change them?

Are you taking some time for self-care? If so, what are you doing? If not, what has prevented you from taking care of yourself?

What are five things you're thankful for this week?

Do you feel like yourself this week?

What would you like to tell your baby this week?

Other Thoughts:

THE FIRST 12 WEEKS: WEEK EIGHT

DATE:

How do you feel this week? Circle one (or several).

Write about how you feel.

Have your basic needs been met this week?

How are you handling depression or any other chronic or situational health-related issues?

Did you have any triggers this week? What are you doing to cope?

What word describes you this week?

Which stage of grief are you in? Describe the stage.

What has been a challenge for you this week?

Where do you find solace?

What are some of your healthy coping strategies? How are you healing?

What are some of your unhealthy coping strategies? How would you like to change those, if you have the desire to change them?

Are you taking some time for self-care? If so, what are you doing? If not, what has prevented you from taking care of yourself?

What are five things you're thankful for this week?

Do you feel like yourself this week?

What would you like to tell your baby this week?

Other Thoughts:

THE FIRST 12 WEEKS: WEEK NINE

DATE:

How do you feel this week? Circle one (or several).

😊 😌 😐 😒 😭 😶

Write about how you feel.

Have your basic needs been met this week?

How are you handling depression or any other chronic or situational
health-related issues?

Did you have any triggers this week? What are you doing to cope?

What word describes you this week?

Which stage of grief are you in? Describe the stage.

What has been a challenge for you this week?

Where do you find solace?

What are some of your healthy coping strategies? How are you healing?

What are some of your unhealthy coping strategies? How would you like to change those, if you have the desire to change them?

Are you taking some time for self-care? If so, what are you doing? If not, what has prevented you from taking care of yourself?

What are five things you're thankful for this week?

Do you feel like yourself this week?

What would you like to tell your baby this week?

Other Thoughts:

THE FIRST 12 WEEKS: WEEK TEN

DATE:

How do you feel this week? Circle one (or several).

Write about how you feel.

Have your basic needs been met this week?

How are you handling depression or any other chronic or situational
health-related issues?

Did you have any triggers this week? What are you doing to cope?

What word describes you this week?

Which stage of grief are you in? Describe the stage.

What has been a challenge for you this week?

Where do you find solace?

What are some of your healthy coping strategies? How are you healing?

What are some of your unhealthy coping strategies? How would you like to change those, if you have the desire to change them?

Are you taking some time for self-care? If so, what are you doing? If not, what has prevented you from taking care of yourself?

What are five things you're thankful for this week?

Do you feel like yourself this week?

What would you like to tell your baby this week?

Other Thoughts:

THE FIRST 12 WEEKS: WEEK ELEVEN

DATE:

How do you feel this week? Circle one (or several).

😊 😌 😐 😒 😭 😶

Write about how you feel.

Have your basic needs been met this week?

How are you handling depression or any other chronic or situational health-related issues?

Did you have any triggers this week? What are you doing to cope?

What word describes you this week?

Which stage of grief are you in? Describe the stage.

What has been a challenge for you this week?

Where do you find solace?

What are some of your healthy coping strategies? How are you healing?

What are some of your unhealthy coping strategies? How would you like to change those, if you have the desire to change them?

Are you taking some time for self-care? If so, what are you doing? If not, what has prevented you from taking care of yourself?

What are five things you're thankful for this week?

Do you feel like yourself this week?

What would you like to tell your baby this week?

Other Thoughts:

THE FIRST 12 WEEKS: WEEK TWELVE

DATE:

How do you feel this week? Circle one (or several).

Write about how you feel.

Have your basic needs been met this week?

How are you handling depression or any other chronic or situational health-related issues?

Did you have any triggers this week? What are you doing to cope?

What word describes you this week?

Which stage of grief are you in? Describe the stage.

What has been a challenge for you this week?

Where do you find solace?

What are some of your healthy coping strategies? How are you healing?

What are some of your unhealthy coping strategies? How would you like to change those, if you have the desire to change them?

Are you taking some time for self-care? If so, what are you doing? If not, what has prevented you from taking care of yourself?

What are five things you're thankful for this week?

Do you feel like yourself this week?

What would you like to tell your baby this week?

Other Thoughts:

IF LOVE COULD HAVE SAVED YOU

If love could have saved you
I would have parted every riptide
Dissolved each cloud of pouring tears
Back into the atmosphere
If love could have saved you.

My heart would have exploded
To see you, newly born, lying on my chest
Tucked underneath a blanket
And around my little finger
If love could have saved you.

Your giggles would have lit up the room
Right beside of your brother's
We'd share kisses and cuddles
In small moments underneath moonlight
If love could have saved you.

Your future would have illuminated the world
Instead, I'm left with shards of could have beens
As you left for your eternal home
Now, two pieces of my heart are in Heaven
If love could have saved you.

If love could have saved you
My mourning heart wouldn't heave in my chest
I wouldn't lay another child to rest
In a piecemeal eulogy on another toilet seat
You're my golden tomorrow
My saving grace in a December daydream
If only love could have saved you.

-

Kaylin R. Staten
April 20, 2021

MONTHLY LETTERS TO YOUR CHILD

Alice:

"How long is forever?"

White Rabbit:

"Sometimes, just one second."

LEWIS CARROLL'S *ALICE IN WONDERLAND*

LETTERS TO YOUR CHILD: MONTH FOUR

DATE:

What do you want to tell your child this month?

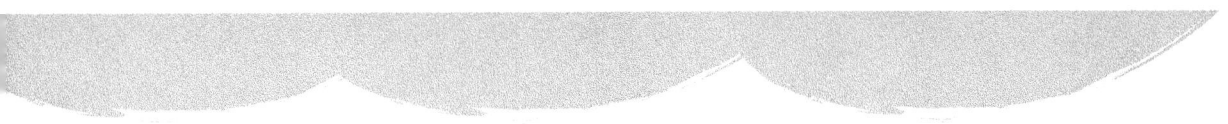

LETTERS TO YOUR CHILD: MONTH FIVE

DATE:

What do you want to tell your child this month?

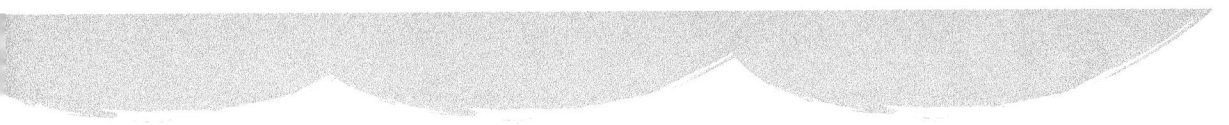

CHAPTER V

LETTERS TO YOUR CHILD: MONTH SIX

DATE:

What do you want to tell your child this month?

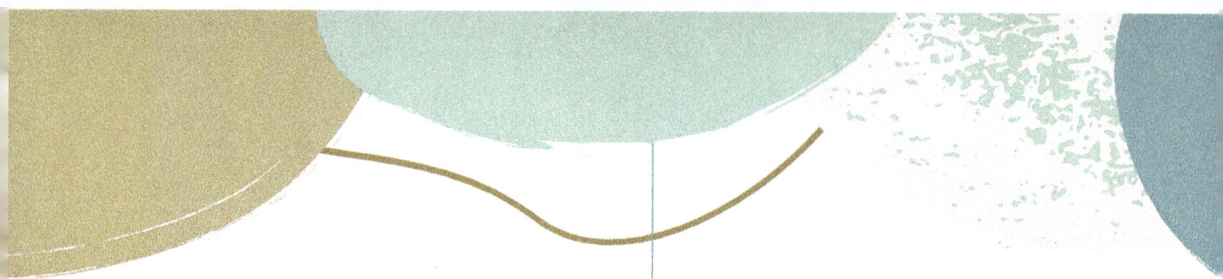

LETTERS TO YOUR CHILD: MONTH SEVEN

DATE:

What do you want to tell your child this month?

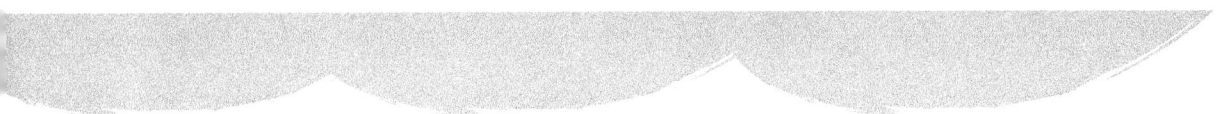

LETTERS TO YOUR CHILD: MONTH EIGHT

DATE:

What do you want to tell your child this month?

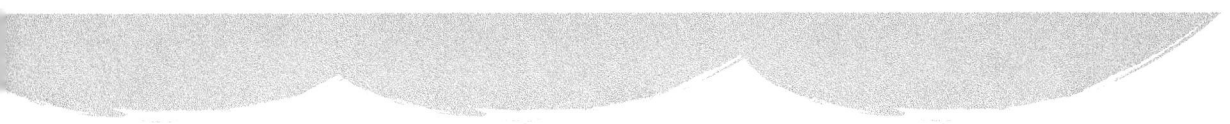

LETTERS TO YOUR CHILD: MONTH NINE

DATE:

What do you want to tell your child this month?

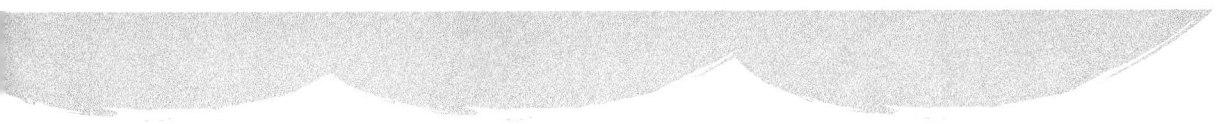

LETTERS TO YOUR CHILD: MONTH TEN

DATE:

What do you want to tell your child this month?

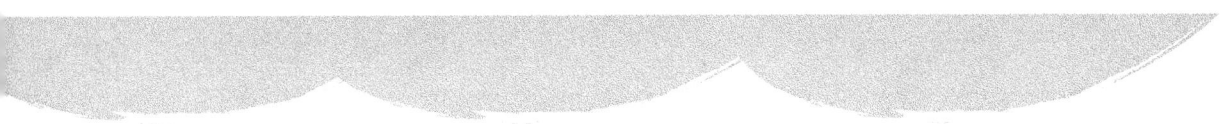

LETTERS TO YOUR CHILD: MONTH ELEVEN

DATE:

What do you want to tell your child this month?

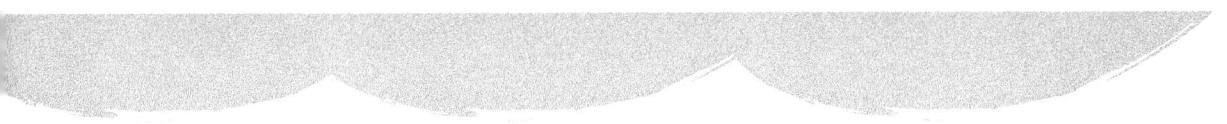

LETTERS TO YOUR CHILD: MONTH TWELVE

DATE:

What do you want to tell your child on his/her due date?

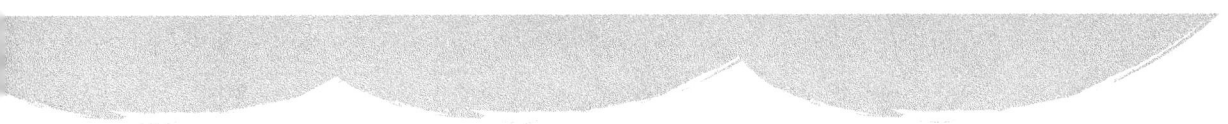

OTHER NOTES

DATE:

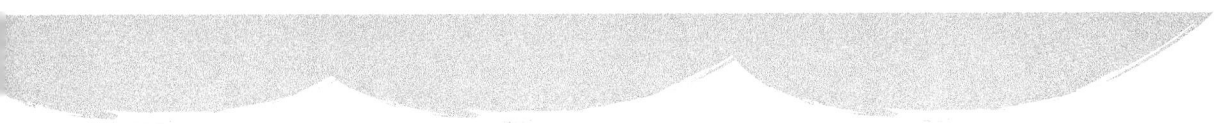

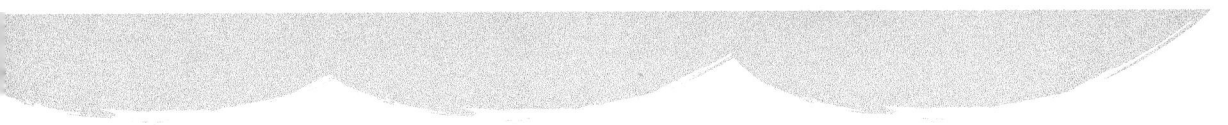

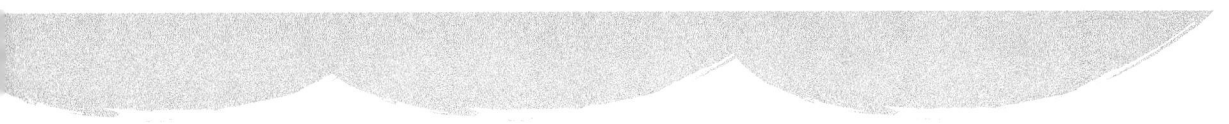

RESURCES

Child Loss Remembrance Day
www.october15th.com

What The Physical Miscarriage Process is Like
www.miscarriageassociation.org.uk/information/miscarriage/the-physical-process

The Miscarriage Association
www.miscarriageassociation.org.uk/your-feelings/your-mental-health +
www.miscarriageassociation.org.uk/information/other-resources

American Pregnancy Association
www.americanpregnancy.org/getting-pregnant/pregnancy-loss/miscarriage-
surviving-emotionally-582

American Psychological Association
www.apa.org/monitor/2012/06/miscarriage

University of Rochester Medical Center:
Women, Pregnancy Loss, and Mental Health Problems
www.urmc.rochester.edu/news/story/women-who-miscarry-have-long-lasting-
mental-health-problems

Study: Depression and Anxiety Following Early Pregnancy Loss
www.ncbi.nlm.nih.gov/pmc/articles/PMC4468887

MGH Center for Women's Mental Health:
Impact of Miscarriages on Partners
www.womensmentalhealth.org/posts/miscarriage-partner

Miscarriage Doula Podcast, Group Sessions, & Resources
www.themiscarriagedoula.co

March of Dimes
www.marchofdimes.org/complications/dealing-with-grief-after-the-death-of-your-
baby.aspx

Miscarriage Matters
www.mymiscarriagematters.org

Miscarriage Hurts
www.miscarriagehurts.com

Return to Zero
www.rtzhope.org

Scan and find more resources here!

How You Feel One Year Later

DATE:

HOW YOU FEEL
ABOUT YOUR LOSS:

THREE WORDS TO DESCRIBE
YOU RIGHT NOW:

HOW YOUR LOSS HAS
CHANGED YOU:

WHAT YOU STILL STRUGGLE WITH:

WHAT ARE YOU GRATEFUL FOR?

www.ingramcontent.com/pod-product-compliance
Lightning Source LLC
Chambersburg PA
CBHW080919100426
42812CB00007B/2327